Original title:
A Brooch for Every Moment

Copyright © 2025 Creative Arts Management OÜ
All rights reserved.

Author: Seraphina Caldwell
ISBN HARDBACK: 978-1-80586-105-8
ISBN PAPERBACK: 978-1-80586-577-3

Enamel and Emotion

A splash of colors bright and bold,
Each piece a story waiting to be told.
With laughter, quirks, and a dash of flair,
They catch the eye with style to spare.

From winking cats to silly ducks,
These charms of joy are pure good luck.
Pin one on shirts or even hats,
Turn mundane days to feline chats.

Timepieces in Brooches

Tick-tock goes the little clock,
Nestled where the laughs unlock.
Time waits not for boring gears,
In jeweled pals, it disappears.

A hummingbird with tiny wings,
Counts down all the silly things.
Each badge a chapter, full of cheer,
With every moment, we hold dear.

Wings of Nostalgia

Fluttering back to days of yore,
A pin of whispers, memories galore.
With butterflies that wink and tease,
They float on laughter, aim to please.

A parrot's beak, a smile that beams,
Reminds us all of childhood dreams.
With every wear, a giggle bright,
Where joy and crazy take their flight.

Dazzling Details

Little gems that shimmer and dance,
Each one a spark of chance romance.
With quirky shapes, they shimmy and sway,
Turning heads in the most charming way.

From donuts to dogs in satin bows,
Life is just better with these shows.
So pin on a smile, let laughter lead,
With details that brighten the world's creed.

Threads of Memory

In a drawer, they sit and wait,
Each clasp, each pin, a small fate.
One's a flower, one a fish,
To wear them all? Oh, what a wish!

Grandma wore them, quite the show,
One fell off, and on her toe.
A sparkly gem, it took flight,
Now it's a tale, shared in delight.

Cherished Adornments

A quirky pin from Auntie Sue,
Worn on shirts, it made quite a view.
With googly eyes and a bright grin,
It was cooler than a winning spin!

Now I wear it, feeling great,
At the office, it's my fate.
With every laugh, I hear its cheer,
Adorning me with memories dear.

Radiance of Realms

A shiny star, from days of yore,
It twinkled bright, but dropped on the floor.
With every step, it would jiggle and jive,
Making my mettle come alive!

A brooch shaped like a giant cake,
Did I wear it? For laughter's sake!
My friends all giggle, what a sight,
In this metal madness, I feel light.

Moments in Metal

A pin shaped like a roaring bear,
It's quite a talker, an odd affair.
When I wear it, I tell a tale,
Of wilderness trips and a comedic fail!

There's one with fruits, all in a row,
Every color, putting on a show.
People stop and give me a nudge,
Laughing about it, no need to grudge!

Crafted by Time

Every pin tells a tale, quite absurd,
Of clumsy moments, it's true, not unheard.
A sparkly flower, a cat with a grin,
It holds all the laughter, where memories begin.

Fastened on jackets, they shimmer and shine,
A broccoli pin? Oh, isn't that divine!
With each little clink, a chuckle's released,
In the world of accessories, humor's the feast.

Glittering Glimpses

A sparkly star on my sock, what a feat!
While I trip on the sidewalk, oh what a treat!
The glimmer of laughter in every misstep,
My closet's a circus, not one of them prepped.

Wearing a fish, oh the smirks that I get,
Friends roll their eyes, but I'm not done yet!
A unicorn dancing, a taco in tow,
With glittery whimsy, I steal every show.

Enchanting Escapades

In a world of pins, we dance like the breeze,
With each little spark, we do just as we please.
A fruit salad brooch mocks my healthy choice,
I wear it with pride, in a much louder voice.

Oh, a penguin on ice skates, so bold and so spry,
As I wobble and giggle, beneath the blue sky.
These pins tell adventures of silly delight,
With every new clasp, my wardrobe takes flight.

Portraits in Pins

Picture this: a dinosaur, decked in bright gold,
A grand story's told, I can hear it unfold.
Each little pin whispers, 'Remember me now?'
An otter with glasses, oh, take a bow!

When friends come to visit, they gaze at my chest,
They point and they chuckle; oh, isn't it best?
From portraits to puns, each moment's a play,
With laughter in pins, we brighten the day.

Artistry in Moments

A shiny gem upon my chest,
Signal of my quirky quest.
Every gathering, a new delight,
Adorning me both day and night.

Laughter spills where jewels align,
Who knew a pin could be so fine?
Each event, a brand-new scene,
Turning mundane into the keen.

A twist of pink, a splash of blue,
Best dressed at the BBQ!
With every clasp, a tale to tell,
Gems and giggles work so well.

Framed in Flair

Sprucing up my outfit grand,
With a little sparkle, oh so planned.
Fastened close, it steals the show,
Who needs a crown when this can glow?

At lunch, my pals shout in glee,
"What's that shiny thing we see?"
I wink and say, "Just a small find,
An accessory that's one of a kind!"

With every clink, it starts to sway,
A rainbow party come what may.
Around my neck or on my sleeve,
We giggle hard, we really believe!

Whimsical Reminders

In a world of ties and suits,
I wear my whimsy like bright boots.
A tiny bird upon my lapel,
It chirps for joy, can you tell?

Each event an oddball chance,
With pins that giggle and dance.
From weddings to the grocery store,
Who knew fun could be so core?

Smiles are stitched on every thread,
They laugh at my pin instead.
Oh days, you turn so hilarious,
My flair's the best, it's so curious!

The Anchor of Memories

A silly smile from the past,
Pinning moments that always last.
At parties, they ask, "What's that?"
I proudly say, "Just my little chat!"

Stuck to my coat, like glue to a shoe,
Each clip's a laugh, oh who knew?
Capture laughter, stitch in time,
Plenty of giggles, all in prime.

From birthdays to odd art shows,
My flair is where the fun life grows.
Anchor down those memories bright,
With a comical catch, life's a delight!

Ephemeral Elegance

A sparkly gem on my old shirt,
Adorning my chaos, it just won't hurt.
Turning my mundane into a grand affair,
Laughing at life, without a single care.

With a butterfly wing on a rainy day,
Who knew a clip could keep blues at bay?
A pop of color on a fleeting breeze,
Life's little laughs are simple to seize.

Keepsakes of the Soul

This quirky pin shaped like a cat,
Stirs up giggles, imagine that!
It's got a story, as it hops and twirls,
In the pocket of life, it joyfully whirls.

Each charm I wear has a tale to tell,
Like my rubber chicken, all giggles and swell.
Collecting laughter, it's my only goal,
These shiny trinkets, they're part of my soul.

The Pin that Tells a Tale

A cupcake pin on a business suit,
Adding a twist, fashionable loot.
It whispers secrets and giggles galore,
As colleagues wonder, what's next in store?

A pirate's hat on a Tuesday morn,
Transforming the office, no one's to scorn.
With every glance, a chuckle ignites,
This pin game's strong, igniting delights!

Ornamenting the Ordinary

A sock pin with stripes, oh what a surprise,
Raising eyebrows and masking sighs.
It sparkles brightly against the drab,
Turning gray days into a fun blab.

My paperclip pin, oh, how it shines,
Insta-coolness, cutting through the lines.
It's just a doodle, yet rich in cheer,
Decorating life, it's what I hold dear!

Shimmering Reflections

In the mirror, there's a dance,
A shiny pin that bids romance.
It laughs at me with every glare,
And whispers tales of silly flair.

I wore it once on a hot dog spree,
It flew off, oh, what a sight to see!
Chasing it down, I lost my shoe,
But hey, that's just what fun can do!

It sparkles bright, a curious tease,
A fashion statement, if you please.
My cat thinks it's a game, oh dear,
Swatting it here, it disappears!

So here's to pins, with funny quirks,
They hold together our silly works.
With every twirl, they bring us cheer,
A little laughter, year by year.

Stories Encased in Gem

A gem of stories, hidden well,
In a quirky shape, it casts a spell.
Once it graced a hat from '89,
Now it's stuck on a sweater line.

That time at lunch, it slipped and fell,
I thought I'd lost my lovely shell.
But there it sat, among the fries,
With ketchup smiles and surprise ties.

Dancing through my tangled hair,
Its sparkle made the zany wear.
Who knew a pin could stir such glee?
It's a wacky version of me!

In every clasp, a tale resides,
Of silly dances and wild rides.
So let it twinkle, let it gleam,
These gem-filled moments, what a dream!

Timeless Fastenings

Fastened tightly, what a sight,
A costume pin, oh, what delight!
It's seen my style, with ups and downs,
From silly smiles to grumpy frowns.

One windy day, it took a chance,
And off it flew—oh, what a dance!
It landed there, on someone's hat,
They wore it proud, imagine that!

A timeless charm, it rusts not fast,
But tries to cling to every blast.
"Please don't remove, I'm having fun!"
It shouts while dancing in the sun.

With every trip, it shows its flair,
A purple gem stuck in my hair.
Though life can twist and turn so wide,
My trusty pin is by my side.

In the Clasp of Memories

In the clasp, memories unfold,
A wacky tale I'm sure you've told.
With sparkles bright from days of yore,
Each moment pinned, we can't ignore.

One time it tried to hitch a ride,
On crazy friends who run and glide.
They danced around, it fell off quick,
To land on my dog's tail—oh, what a trick!

Underneath the couch, a mystery,
Worn by the cat, a history.
Together we've laughed, we've been so bold,
In every shimmer, our tales are told.

So let the pins perform their art,
In every clasp, you'll find a heart.
With laughter bright, we'll always cheer,
For every moment, bring the gear!

Preserving the Past

In a drawer, old treasures hide,
Buckle and snaps—fancy and wide.
Liberated from mothballs, they gleam,
Like a vintage photo caught in a dream.

Grandma's pin from a long-lost fling,
Worn by a cat who loved to cling.
A romance faded, but the laughter stayed,
These little gems have got it made.

Glistening Gatherings

Oh, look—everyone's bling is bright,
Cousin Joe's tie pin? Quite the sight!
A gathering of odd, mismatched style,
Sequins and gems, sure to beguile.

A brooch here, a pin there, what a fête!
Who knew Aunt Sally could accessorize so great?
We twirl and giggle, having a blast,
In this sparkling chaos, all good times amassed.

The Essence of Elegance

Dressed to the nines, that's the goal,
With shiny baubles, we take a stroll.
But wait—a flower pin fits so wrong,
It's a laugh parade—the fashion throng!

A feather here, a sparkle there,
Did I just wear a parrot's hair?
Elegance, they say, is a classy affair,
But I just aim for the funny stare.

Memory Pins and Inspirations

Each pin a tale, a tickled mind,
Of times and places—oh, so unrefined!
The wobbly bobble that used to sway,
Sure sparked a giggle at the dance buffet.

A map of memories, all safe and neat,
Like a treasure hunt but with dancing feet.
A pin for the laughter that flows like wine,
Who knew nostalgia could also be divine?

Jewels of Time

In a drawer, shiny things lay,
Spinning tales of a goofy day.
Each gem a chuckle, each clasp a grin,
Moments of laughter, where do I begin?

Oh, that pendant from last year's spree,
Riding a llama, just you and me.
With sparkles that twinkle like our fun,
A dorky adventure, oh what a run!

Broccoli carbonara, oh what a find,
A pin reminds me, we were unrefined.
With each silly trinket, memories bloom,
In this treasure chest, laughter resumes.

Adornments of Emotion

A bracelet, just a touch too tight,
Squeezes my wrist but feels so right.
With charms that jiggle, and jokes on the side,
Each trinket a chuckle, a whimsical ride.

Earrings shaped like oversized fries,
Joking around, much to our surprise.
Every twirl, a story to tell,
Of goofy escapades where we fell.

A necklace with cupcakes, sweet as can be,
Reminding me of parties, just you and me.
We laugh 'til we cry, through thick and thin,
In these silly adornments, we're bound to win.

Keepsakes of the Heart

In this box of silly delights,
Live keys to our wild and wacky nights.
A pin shaped like a cat with shades,
Unveiling laughter, where fun never fades.

Oh, the time when we danced with glee,
Wearing socks that were far beyond tacky.
Each bead and bauble sparkles with grace,
Moments that bring a smile to my face.

With heart-shaped tokens and charms so bright,
Reminding us of that epic food fight.
Keepsakes we wear with humor and flair,
Brought together by joy, love, and care.

Trinkets of Memory

A quirky pin from a roadside stand,
Sparkling laughter when you hold my hand.
With memories wrapped in shiny threads,
Each piece whispers what life truly spreads.

A charm shaped like a pizza slice,
We'd dine together, oh, how nice!
Silly moments stuck to our hearts,
Garlands of joy, where giggling starts.

In pockets of fabric and corners of drawers,
Hide laughter and stories, treasures galore!
These trinkets of memory, bright and bold,
Craft a tale of us, worth more than gold.

Pins of Significance

On my coat, a flower spins,
A pin that makes me grin.
It sparkles bright, a sunny hue,
Worn on days when I feel blue.

A fish that flops, it dances near,
To catch attention, I hold dear.
It wiggles just to make me laugh,
In dull meetings, it's my craft.

An owl that blinks with googly eyes,
In every chat, it makes me wise.
With each tale, it flaps its wings,
A master of the silly things.

So many pins, so little time,
Collecting stories, oh so prime.
In every clasp, a tale's begun,
Pin pals unite, we're so much fun!

The Stories We Wear

A tiny cat, with yarn in tow,
Chasing dreams where no one goes.
Sewn on shirts, it's quite absurd,
The best way to be heard!

An ice cream cone, a melting treat,
On my dress, it can't be beat.
Drips of color, syrupy sweet,
Reminding me when life's a feat.

A paper airplane, just for flair,
Zooming past, I've got no care.
It flies with ease through crowd and din,
Who knew that life could be so kin?

With these quirks, I strut my stuff,
In every laugh, the road gets rough.
Each badge I wear, a joke, a jest,
Life's a show, and I'm the best!

Moments Captured in Metal

Captured moments in shiny form,
A taco pin starts the gourmet storm.
With toppings bright, it teases taste,
Conversations flow, never a waste.

A pair of socks, mismatched delight,
On my bag, they feel just right.
They giggle as we walk around,
In this silliness, joy is found.

A superhero, with cape unfurled,
Battles boredom in our world.
With every clasp, a chuckle springs,
In life's parade, we wear the bling.

These moments shine, a laugh we share,
In each pin, a story's flare.
So round them up, let's celebrate,
With every wink, we've sealed our fate!

Emblems of Tomorrow

Future dreams in silver thread,
A robot dances, full of dread.
It's got a glitch, but who could tell?
On my jacket, it fits so well.

A lightning bolt, it zings and zaps,
This one's for good and silly claps.
Every flash, a giggle starts,
In every wink, we share our hearts.

A rainbow sprout, with colors bold,
On my shirt, it never gets old.
Shining bright, it steals the show,
In a world of gray, it helps us grow.

These emblems bright, our future shows,
In every laugh, our kindness glows.
As we move forward, pins held high,
Together we'll let laughter fly!

Artistry in Each Gesture

In a world of pins and clips,
I sport a piece that truly quips.
It winks and twirls with every sway,
Making mundane the highlight of the day.

With a chicken dance and twinkling flair,
My jewelry speaks, it's quite a pair.
Each gesture gleams, a laugh or two,
My outfit grand, yet still brand new.

Ribbons and tags, a playful spree,
Each twinkle begs, 'Come laugh with me!'
My flair's a joy, a foolish jest,
In the grandest ball, I'm truly dressed.

From the fridge to the finest cheer,
Every moment shines, oh dear!
With jokes and winks, it's quite the sight,
In my wardrobe, laughter takes flight.

Sentiments in Silver

A silver pin of somewhat odd,
Picks up the mood, that's the job!
With every glance, I giggle loud,
It's really something, I feel quite proud.

Dancing on my blouse, it plays a role,
Winking at friends, making them whole.
With puns engraved, it's quite the feat,
My fashion statement, utterly neat.

When life gets tough, and hugs are few,
This shiny friend knows just what to do.
It sparkles and shines with a cheeky laugh,
Turning frowns into a joyful craft.

So here's the truth, in a silver hue,
Adorning my heart with each silly cue.
In every gesture, a sentiment bright,
A giggle of joy, it's pure delight.

The Dance of Adornment

With every hop and skip I make,
My jewels wink, they never break.
Dancing lightly, I swirl around,
My accessories speak without a sound.

Feathers and gems, a quirky blast,
In this rhythm, I have a blast.
The necklaces giggle, the earrings swing,
In my dance of joy, they leap and cling.

Each pin I wear tells a funny tale,
From mishaps to quirks, they never fail.
In laughter's embrace, they find their place,
This jig of joy, a soft embrace.

So join the dance, oh come and see,
The playful joy, a jubilee.
With adornments bright, life's a parade,
In every twirl, new moments made.

Symbols of Rhythmic Days

In colors bold, my badges shine,
Marking moments, turning in line.
A silly grin with every clasp,
Each day's rhythm in a playful grasp.

From breakfast blues to coffee buzz,
These little charms, they sure are a fuzz.
With laughter leading the merry dance,
In a world so grand, I take a chance.

Each quirky piece a story tells,
Of mishaps bright and jangly bells.
A button here, a charm placed right,
Every symbol brings pure delight.

So wear your treasures, make them sing,
In daily rhythms, let laughter ring.
With silly moments, life takes flight,
Each day adorned, forever bright.

Trinkets of Experience

Cheap trinkets on my chest,
I wear them with some zest.
A bottle cap, a paper clip,
Fashion choices make me flip.

Button from a shirt once worn,
On my jacket, it is borne.
A sprightly charm from a cereal box,
I strut around like I'm a fox.

A badge from a school that I forgot,
Worn with pride, though I was caught.
These treasures tell each tale I tell,
With every jingle, laughter swells.

In each piece, I find the fun,
In quirky things, I feel like one.
Glitter, sparkles, wild and free,
Oh, how delightful they can be!

Tokens of the Heart

A gum wrapper from a date,
Secured to me, it feels so fate.
A twisty tie from that coffee shop,
I flaunt it like I'm on the top.

Old keys, they're not a thing I lose,
They hang around like old news.
Like tokens, they jingle with glee,
Reminders of who I used to be.

A smiley face, made of clay,
Dangles on my coat all day.
Heart-shaped rocks and mismatched pins,
Each one's a laugh, where fun begins.

With laughter stitched into this cloth,
I wear my heart on a loose froth.
Such charms bring cheer, you see it's true,
Tokens of joy in varied hue.

Captured in Curves

With curves that bind and clasp,
I wear them all; please, take a gasp!
A circle from the old dog's tag,
An ice cream scoop, it makes me brag.

Curly fries, they're a mystic charm,
Attached to my coat, oh so warm.
A spiral of foam from a whipped treat,
Each curve sends giggles to my seat.

The jester's cap, bright like summer,
I wear it, oh yes, what a bummer!
Yet all in jest, my heart takes flight,
Captured in curves, a pure delight.

In laughter's hold, I twist and spin,
A life of whimsy, where to begin?
Each curve tells tales of fun days past,
In joyous loops, forever cast.

Elegance of the Everyday

I wear a fork, but make no fuss,
Paired with a spoon, just for us.
A rubber band, quite the chic,
My style's unique, so to speak.

An old shoelace with a bow,
It dangles down, stealing the show.
With dignity, I bring out the whim,
In everyday life, I'll dance and swim.

A lighter, a whistle, what a mix!
For elegance, I know the tricks.
My mom's old earring, one in a set,
It jingles softly, you can bet.

Oh, life is grand with pieces so sweet,
An upscale look that can't be beat.
In laughter and grace, I proudly strut,
Finding elegance in every cut!

Sparkles in the Seconds

In the drawer, trinkets jive,
With bright glimmers, they come alive.
A chicken, a seahorse, all in a swirl,
Fashion statements for every twirl.

Clip it to hats or to shirts so bold,
Each tiny piece has a story told.
Glancing at life, we can't help but grin,
When a butterfly lands on a cheeky chin.

In a pocket or purse, they dance and play,
Mixing and matching, making our day.
With a wink and a nod, they share their flair,
Who knew a pin could capture such air?

So gather those gems, let the laughter soar,
These shiny delights, we simply adore.
With a wink and a giggle, let joy commence,
In this wild world, no moments are dense.

Heirlooms of the Now

An old tie clasp, a pin with a cat,
Every piece carries a story or spat.
With a flick of the wrist, bring past to today,
These heirlooms of fun, in a clownish display.

A button collects dust but dreams to be seen,
Worn with pride, and maybe a bean.
The stories we tell in shiny arrays,
Each piece whispers laughs from long-ago days.

Tangled in hair or all stuck to a shoe,
Life's little quirks in a dazzling view.
With laughter we share, our treasures reflect,
The humor in life, we happily select.

So let's dress ourselves in nostalgia's parade,
With whimsical charm that never will fade.
An heirloom today can spark a good cheer,
In moments of laughter, our hearts will steer.

Tokens of Treasured Days

A paperclip dressed like a dragonfly,
Holds secrets of laughter, oh my, oh my!
With mismatched charms and buttons galore,
Each trinket's a giggle from days that we wore.

In pockets they nest, waiting their turn,
To shine and to sparkle, to teach us to learn.
A feather, a thimble, a spark of surprise,
With silly reflections, our memories rise.

The joys in the little, the giggles that cling,
Tokens of moments that make our hearts sing.
So grab that lost earring, let's twirl it about,
In the rhythm of laughter, there's never a doubt.

Each pin has its purpose, so uniquely made,
In the treasure of life, they're never delayed.
Let's don our odd bits, and frolic with glee,
For every small token whispers: "Be free!"

The Weight of Small Wonders

In the cupboard of quirks, the tiniest finds,
Whispers of mischief in colorful binds.
A matchbox car stuck on a coat,
Sends us to laughter with every note.

With paperclips forming a disco ball,
We celebrate moments, both big and small.
A rubber duck strutting on someone's lap,
Each piece brings a chuckle, a giggly clap.

These wonders of small, though weightless they sway,
Can hold all our secrets from yesterday.
Worn with a wink, they bring joy to the hour,
Transforming the mundane into sparkling power.

So gather the odd and the strange from each shelf,
Let's dress for fun, not just for ourselves.
With the weight of such wonders, how can we frown?
These tokens of joy surely never drown.

Shimmering Reminiscences

In the drawer, treasures lie,
Glimmers of days gone by,
A pin that saves my coffee stains,
And one that hides the holiday gains.

A sparkly star from last year's fling,
Worn with pride at a wedding ring.
Oh, the things I've pinned with glee,
Like my cat's hair and an old car key.

Memory lane is quite a trek,
With every pin, I don't regret.
I laugh at moments, big and small,
Decorated tales hang on my wall.

So here's to whims, the shiny and bright,
Each little trinket feels just right.
For every belly laugh and sigh,
A shiny piece to hold on high.

A Cluster of Memories

On my coat, a carnival flair,
A bell that jingles, bright and rare.
A pin from last year's Halloween,
With a ghost that's hardly seen!

A floral piece from Grandma's days,
Remembering her quirky ways.
A burst of colors, here and there,
Laughing at style with such a flair.

Each pin a verse, each gem a word,
Some are lovely, others absurd.
Like a glob of glue from an old craft spree,
What a sight they are to see!

A little chaos up on my chest,
Each cluster shines, and I feel blessed.
Wearing memories, I chuckle with cheer,
For what's life without a bit of weird?

Each Pin Tells a Story

Upon my lapel, a quirky duck,
Waddling proud with a dash of luck.
Next, a heart that's half undone,
From a date that fell flat, not much fun.

An owl that hoots on a day so bright,
Provoking laughter, a joyful sight.
Each charm a whisper of past delight,
Tales that twinkle through day and night.

A thimble from my failed sewing spree,
A not-so-subtle nod to my artistry.
Every pin, a giggle trapped,
In a sparkling story, sweetly wrapped.

So here I stand with flair and fun,
A gallery of moments, one by one.
A sprinkle of laughter wherever I roam,
With pins like these, I'm never alone!

The Weight of a Moment

A shiny turtle weighing down my vest,
It carries secrets I can't digest.
Another flower, petals askew,
Reminds me of mornings I nearly flew.

A pin shaped like a tiny phone,
Texts from friends? Oh, how they've grown!
And a crown that sparkles but feels so light,
Named after victories we share at night.

Silly pieces cling to my pride,
Each a laugh, a joy, a ride.
From toddler tantrums to grown-up woes,
The weight of moments only humor knows.

So, I'll keep wearing this jumbled haul,
Each trinket a story, a hearty call.
With laughter's embrace, I stride through time,
For joy, after all, is the best rhyme.

Flair for the Fantastic

On a coat, a sparkly pin,
Made of plastic – what a win!
Funky shapes that twist and twirl,
Perfect for a silly girl.

Glitter castles, dancing frogs,
A unicorn with tiny logs.
Each one tells a goofy tale,
Wearing them, I never fail!

When the world is feeling blue,
I find joy in every hue.
With a winking smiley face,
I bring laughter to this place.

So clip it here, and pin it there,
A badge of laughs, I proudly wear.
In a world so unimpressed,
My flair is truly the best!

Tokens of Yesterday

Grandma's fossil, chipped but sweet,
Worn with love, it can't be beat.
An old key from a box so grand,
Unlocks laughter, isn't life planned?

Vintage dots that spin and glint,
Add a chuckle with a hint.
Each one holds a story old,
Of silly days and laughter bold.

A pinch, a poke, a clever tease,
With these pins, I aim to please.
Every memory, a funny cheer,
They sparkle bright, bringing near.

So wear your treasures, blend them right,
In this whimsical fashion fight!
Each token shows the joy I know,
With humor dancing in the glow!

The Brooch of Now

A chicken dance, I wear it proud,
It makes me laugh, attracts a crowd.
Jellybeans and glitter bombs,
For every bump, the humor calms.

Imagine peacocks made of silk,
With tiny bows and shiny milk.
Each pin says, 'Let's have some fun!'
I wear them all – there's never one!

On Mondays too, with sleepy eyes,
A sassy wink, oh how it flies!
Wearing humor through the days,
In a joyful, funny haze.

So join me now and grab a pin,
Let's giggle wide, let's spin and grin!
With every clip, a laugh we'll sow,
In this silly show of 'now.'

Dazzling Reflections

Reflecting giggles in each piece,
With sparkly gems that never cease.
A fish that swims, a shoe that moves,
Each pin a joke that always grooves.

A rubber ducky, silly grin,
It quacks along, letting joy in.
With colors bright, a playful dance,
These dazzling gems give life a chance.

Every clasp, a wink and nod,
In my closet, they form a squad.
Mix and match, come have a ball,
Dazzling charm for one and all!

Life's a stage, I wear the show,
With every pin, I steal the glow.
Who knew such fun could be so grand,
Reflecting laughter, hand in hand!

Crafted Connections

On a jacket, a shiny fly,
Winks at everyone passing by.
Friends gather 'round for a cheer,
Gossiping with our pins near.

A silver cat with a sly grin,
Whispers secrets, let the fun begin.
Twinkling under café light,
Each pin tells tales of delight.

Button here and ribbon there,
Unlock laughter everywhere.
A slip of flair, a wink of eye,
With our pins, we float on by.

So gather round, let's make a fuss,
Clip on joy, no need to rush.
With each piece, we start anew,
Crafted connections in our crew.

Stitches of Sentiment

A flamingo in a tutu stands,
Balancing on the fabric lands.
Every stitch with tales we wear,
Life's patchwork leaps, a comedic flair.

Oh look, a donut on my sleeve,
Bright and silly, who'd believe?
Every pin, a quirky find,
Heartfelt giggles left behind.

A vintage car, a wobbly wheel,
On our outfits, fun we feel.
The stitches bind us, here we are,
Each silly piece, a shining star.

With laughter shared, we strut and spray,
Our allegiance to humor on display.
With every laugh and silly trend,
Stitches of sentiment never end.

A Pin for Every Purpose

A cactus dons a sparkly crown,
On my lapel, it won't back down!
Pointy but it gathers cheer,
A prickly friend that brings us near.

A gnome with a bright red cap,
Sitting snug, no chance of a nap.
Each pin an ally in our quest,
To add some whimsy with the best.

A donut pin, the sweetest bite,
Glazes sparkling, oh what a sight!
Just when life gets a bit low,
A pin can help the laughter flow.

So raise a toast with pins held high,
In our collection, we rely.
For every moment, big or shy,
A pin awaits to make you fly.

Sparkling Segments of Time

A clock that laughs, what good is time?
With every tick, it loves to chime.
Seconds sparkle, laughter flies,
As tiny moments break the skies.

The banana peel, a funny catch,
On my coat, brings us a match.
Every moment's a silly rhyme,
When nestled in our sparkling time.

The unicorn struts without a care,
A whimsical ride, let's not compare.
In this world, let's tiptoe and dance,
With pins in hand, we take a chance.

The past is bright, the future gleams,
Each laughing gem fuels our dreams.
Sparkling segments, witty delight,
In every moment, joy ignites.

Ornaments of Life's Journey

In the drawer, a wonder waits,
A shiny piece, our fate creates.
It sparkles bright, a fancy fling,
Who knew metal could make us sing?

Clip it on with a wobbly grin,
Who knew fashion was a spin?
It flutters here, it skips a beat,
Like a dance with two left feet!

A crown for days that seem so drab,
A laugh that pulls from every grab.
From birthdays to the rainy days,
It highlights joy in clever ways!

So if life's dull, just take a cue,
Pin on some fun, a little too!
Each moment dressed in shiny cheer,
Transforming woes into a beer!

Echoes of Elegance

A sparkle here, a twizzle there,
It's pretty chaos, we declare!
It tells a tale of grand affairs,
And awkward hugs amid the stares.

Pearls and gems, a playful crew,
Each one has something fun to do.
Sputtering laughs in the quiet night,
Like a light show that's out of sight!

In pockets deep or on a dress,
A twinkling hope, a true success.
With every clasp, it joins the ride,
A trusty friend, right by your side!

So wear it grand, or just a bit,
Let elegance have a quirky skit.
In moments lost or moments found,
A little joy that spins around!

Fastened Emotions

A little clip, a tiny twist,
Wrapped in giggles, it can't be missed.
It holds the stories, wild and sweet,
Emotions pinned, it can't be beat!

A badge of honor? Or just for flair?
In every capacity, without a care.
From sleepy days to fancy places,
It brings together our funny faces!

It knows our hearts, the ups and downs,
The times we laughed, the times we frowns.
Fastened tight on sleeves or hats,
It's like friendship - how about that!

So pin it on and join the fun,
An outfit's friend, a race to run.
Each moment cherished in a snap,
With homage paid to life's little map!

The Spark of Significance

It dangles bright, just like my hopes,
A glint of fun, with twisty ropes.
From silly pics to golden dreams,
It's the laughter sewn in our seams!

A quirky piece, a ticklish find,
It mirrors back our silly mind.
From grandma's tales to midnight schemes,
It fits just right in all our themes!

So clasp it on, embrace the flair,
A shiny wink, without a care.
Moments crafted, both near and far,
Like shooting stars, our own bizarre!

Let each sparkle tell a story true,
Of giggles shared or something new.
For in this life, a little glitz,
Makes every memory a perfect fit!

Collecting Fleeting Whispers

Tiny trinkets gather dust,
A clip for moments filled with rust.
Each one tells a quirky tale,
Of outings that went off the rail.

Brought a charm from a lost shoe,
Or a button—who knew it was blue?
In pockets deep, they reside,
With memories that giggle and glide.

Scavenging joy from every seam,
These oddments fuel the silliest dream.
A key that fits no locked door,
But opens laughter, that's for sure.

So here's to the silly and small,
Each little piece—its own call.
They wink and cheer with delight,
Collecting whispers, day and night.

Treasures of Transition

A tangled mess of random bits,
The treasures found in thrift store skits.
From paper clips to fruit-shaped pins,
Each is a laugh, where the fun begins.

This rubber duck with a crooked grin,
Recalls that time when we all lost a kin.
A sandwich press shaped like a car,
Takes us back; oh, how bizarre!

In the shuffle of life's endless quest,
We hoard the laughs, forget the rest.
Every oddity, a treasure chest,
Bringing humor on a wild quest.

So gather 'round, my eclectic crew,
With mismatched gems from me to you.
For transitions may bring ups and downs,
But laughs stay bright, without the frowns.

Jewels in the Journey

On the road, we find it all,
A shiny coin, a bouncy ball.
Each one a jewel that brims with fun,
A sparkling nod to what we've done.

A sock that lost its mate somewhere,
Is a whimsical trophy, if you dare.
In the journey, let's not forget,
The silly finds we won't regret.

A forgotten toy from days gone by,
Brings back the laughter, oh my, oh my!
Through ups and downs, we carry on,
Collecting smiles, till the dawn.

So cherish the gems that life bestows,
With laughter blooming like bright, wild rose.
For every step is a dance, a play,
More treasures found along the way.

Charmed by the Present

Wrapped in chaos, a gem appears,
A cereal toy that tickles the years.
Who knew that joy could fit so small,
In shiny wrappers, we find our call?

A plastic spoon from last year's feast,
Serves as a trophy for the beast.
Every item, a giggle-packed prize,
Winks and whispers of past goodbyes.

From tangled threads to lost old shirts,
In every corner, silliness flirts.
Let's gather the past with playful spark,
As we navigate life's funny dark.

Oh, charmed by the now, let's dance and play,
With quirks and giggles lighting the way.
For in every moment, a chuckle awaits,
Just waiting there behind all the plates.

Whispering Pins

A tiny pin upon my chest,
Looks quite smart, I must confess.
But when I peek, it winks back,
And laughs at all my style's the knack.

In meetings clear, it starts to sway,
Distracts my boss, oh what a play!
It twirls around, a cheeky thing,
My fashion sense, it starts to swing.

Be still my heart, it's time to shine,
With every glance, it steals the line.
Poking fun, it knows the score,
A jest for all, forever more!

Adorning the Journey

Upon my hat, a charm so bright,
Each trip we take, it takes a flight.
With every bump, it hops and plays,
And shimmies as we wind our ways.

In bus and train, it steals the show,
It tickles folks from top to toe.
"Where'd you get that?" they all inquire,
I say, "It makes the trip inspired!"

From beach to mountains, here it goes,
Collecting stories, laughs, and woes.
My trusty pin, oh what a friend,
In every journey, fun won't end!

Echoes of Elegance

A shimmer fox pinned to my sleeve,
With tales of mischief, it believes.
It slides with grace, but oh so sly,
In fancy halls, it's quite the spy.

At parties grand, it starts to tease,
Whispers of secrets that you can't seize.
It giggles low, with each remark,
Stealing glances, leaving its mark.

In classy circles, it's the toast,
Of every gathering, it's the boast.
With every wiggle, charm unfolds,
Echoes of laughter, stories told!

Sentimental Sparkles

A twinkling gem on grandma's coat,
Feels like her hugs, a love to gloat.
It nods hello to every friend,
With memories shared, a love to send.

At every wedding, it starts to shine,
With whispered vows, it's most divine.
It sways and sparkles, knows no bounds,
Connecting hearts through joyful sounds.

In every box, its stories bloom,
Adorning days, it scents the room.
With laughter bright and smiles wide,
A heartfelt gem, with love as guide!

Symbolism in Silver

In silver's gleam, a story's told,
A quirk of fashion, oh so bold.
It dances lightly on your chest,
A spark of whimsy, simply the best.

With every wink, it twists and sways,
A jesting charm in bright arrays.
You clasp it tight, it gives a nod,
Says 'Life's a laugh,' with no facade.

A little fox, a chubby bear,
It announces purpose everywhere.
In meetings drab, it steals the show,
Turning dull chats to a lively flow.

So wear it proud and wear it well,
Each piece a tale, a giggling spell.
In every moment, let it shine,
A badge of humor, truly divine.

The Charm of Remembrance

A tiny frog hops on my sleeve,
What little charm, I do believe!
It squeaks of memories tucked away,
In laughter's light, it loves to play.

I pin it on for folks to see,
'Why yes, it's quirky as can be!'
It nudges friends to start to grin,
Celebrating every whim and spin.

Old tales resurface with each glance,
The dorky pin makes hearts entrance.
With teasing jests, we share a past,
A charming jest that will always last.

So let's adorn our lives with glee,
These memories wrapped in jubilee.
With each sweet smile, we'll reenact,
The art of fun—now that's a fact!

Twinkling Testaments

Oh twinkle, twinkle, metal bright,
A happy trinket, pure delight.
It sparkles tales of joy and jest,
A treasure found in a silly quest.

A cat, a cloud, a pair of shoes,
Each charm's a laugh, it just enthuse.
A gentle tug on life's parade,
With every glance, your mood's remade.

It tickles fancies, brings a cheer,
Like laughter shared with friends so dear.
In every clasp, a wink is found,
As joy and whimsy whirl around.

So shine, you trinket, bold and free,
In every wink, a jubilee.
Our spirits high, our hearts aglow,
Each sparkling charm, a fun-filled show!

Emblems of Eternity

In odd designs, we find a jest,
Each piece a badge, a curious quest.
From winking eyes to silly hats,
Who knew we'd wear such quirky chats?

They tell of nights both wild and free,
With every catch, a laugh, you see.
A heart that giggles on my lapel,
Reminds me snugly of tales to tell.

Oh, what fun to own the silly,
For laughter brightens up the chilly!
With every sparkle, we declare,
Life's too short, so let's beware!

So pin your tales, let humor reign,
In every moment, joy's the gain.
These emblems of a life lived loud,
Are stories sung, beautiful and proud.

Moments Encased in Metal

In a drawer, they sit and wait,
Each one a tale to narrate.
A quirky smile, a tiny dance,
Who knew they'd bring such a chance?

A pin from grandma, worn askew,
Once lost, now found, who knew it grew?
Life's little slips, a laugh or two,
Oh, the stories, if they only knew!

Buttoned up with flair and glee,
A fashion statement, wild and free.
Metallic memories stacked in rows,
To remind us how life ebbs and flows.

So grab a piece, a sparkly delight,
And wear it wrong with all your might.
For every moment, big or small,
A jester's charm brightens it all.

The Clutches of the Past

In the attic, treasures lie,
A pin of pizza, oh my, oh my!
Someone's charm from days of yore,
Did they think it'd start a war?

A lopsided cat with an odd, green eye,
Pinned on a vest, oh how we sigh.
Worn with pride, a wobbly thing,
What was it for? I just can't cling.

Brooches worn to every prom,
What a time, eccentric and calm.
Each clasped memory feels so bold,
As we giggle at the tales retold.

Hold tight to these emblems rare,
Awkward fashion, yet we don't care.
For in the laughter, we find our way,
Each piece a tale, come what may!

Captured Charm

A tiny owl with wobbly wings,
Wears a look that joyously sings.
Stuck on a coat during a blizzard,
How did it survive that weird lizard?

Roses and ribbons that never fade,
Sewing pins lost, oh, what a parade!
Each one's a story, a comedic twist,
Glimpses of moments we can't resist.

Bobbles and jingles on a bland old dress,
Style may be questionable, I guess.
But with each brooch, a playful charm,
Life's ironies surround us, keeping us warm.

So let's adorn with laughter in mind,
And see what old memories we can find.
For every moment, there's a pin to attach,
To remind us to cherish, and love every patch.

The Elegance of Experience

In a dress with flair, quite a sight,
A shiny pin took flight,
It slipped and slid, oh what a fuss,
Now it's the star, what's the rush?

A clip gone rogue, a shimmy and jig,
It sparked a dance, oh how big!
With laughs all around, we'll toast the day,
To charms that lead us astray!

A formal lunch, a casual grin,
That silly thing, where to begin?
It bounced right off and danced away,
We'll chase it down, hip-hip-hooray!

So let's adorn with quirky taste,
For memories made, we'll never waste,
In all the fun, an outfit's flair,
With every giggle, show you care!

Clusters of Hope

A garden full of gems so bright,
With mismatched stones that just feel right,
Some are silly, others grand,
All hold dreams we've lightly planned.

A little daisy, a ladybug,
Together they made quite the snug hug,
With every wink, they gleam and glow,
Who knew a brooch could put on a show?

At parties pale, with laughter loud,
Our funky pins make us proud,
They chat and shine, a runway flair,
What a cluster of fun to wear!

So gather round, everyone,
With moments shared and laughter spun,
In style we trust, with charms bestowed,
Making memories as we go!

Embraces in Enamel

The colors swirl in merry delight,
A silly heart pin took flight,
It twirls and flips, a show of glee,
"Catch me if you can!" it cries with glee.

My collar's joy, it darts around,
A winking star snags the sound,
A playful air, a wobbly swing,
Who knew such things could do their thing?

With every hug and every cheer,
Those round enamel smiles appear,
They fit so snug, it seems quite grand,
Fashion laughter, hand in hand!

So let's parade these charms anew,
In fun and folly, we'll break through,
These quirky things, they seem to know,
The brighter moments steal the show!

Charmed Encounters

At every corner, gems collide,
With stories bold, they don't abide,
A clip that hangs by threads so frail,
Its tales of mishaps, never pale.

With every outfit, a tale's set free,
That zany charm on me, oh me!
It nudges folks to laugh and play,
In this wild ride, we'll sway away.

A winking cat, a dancing bee,
Together they make quite the spree,
With every jingle, the hearts collide,
A fashion fest, our goofy guide!

So bring the laughter, spread the cheer,
With every pin, we hold so dear,
In bling we trust, our style we flaunt,
In shiny charms, we all will haunt!

The Essence Enshrined

In the drawer, treasures hide,
Sparkling tales, full of pride.
A lizard pin, bright and green,
Who knew it would cause a scene?

Each clasp a story, oh what fun,
A cat that dances in the sun.
When friends come over, let's wear them right,
Expecting giggles, oh what a sight!

At parties, who needs a dress?
With pins like these, I must confess.
They steal the show, and make me grin,
Let the brooch wars, oh, let them begin!

So here's to clasping, without a doubt,
A history lesson, fun to shout.
Let's wear them proudly, and take a bow,
With every sparkle, let's wow the crowd!

Glittering Moments

On my lapel, a quirky bee,
It buzzes soft, yet makes me glee.
Friends come over, they can't ignore,
"Is that a bug?!" Laughs roar galore.

A fish that swims upside-down,
What a gem to wear in town!
"Catch of the day," they say with cheer,
A swimming lesson, let's draw near!

At weddings, I'm the funny one,
Adorning feathers that look like fun.
"Did you lose a parrot?" they inquire,
In rib-tickling moments, I never tire.

So here's to pins, so wild and free,
Each story shared, a jubilee.
With laughter bright, let's make a toast,
To shimmering memories, we love the most!

Ties that Shimmer

A quirky horse, with a tiny hat,
Rides on my coat, what's up with that?
"Is it a ranch or a fair?" they jest,
As smiles spread wide, inviting the best.

An octopus in a twinkling hue,
"Do you swim too?" I hear them coo.
What tales I spin in this hilarious dress,
Oh, the moments I won't suppress!

A starfish with bling joins the cabaret,
"I've got sea legs!" it seems to say.
Why wear plain when you can shine?
With laughter blooming, oh, how divine!

Ties that shimmer, tales unfold,
Punny pins, pure entertainment gold.
Let's clasp these memories, in quirky lines,
With fun accessories, that help us shine!

Classic Keepsakes

An old-school pin, with a modern twist,
Turns heads fast; it can't be missed.
"Is that a clock?" they giggle and squeal,
Just ticking loud, it knows the deal!

A castle perched atop my chest,
"Ready for a royal quest?"
Noble moments we play pretend,
Every laugh, it seems, won't end.

With a quirky beaver, busy and bright,
"Is it for the dam?" they laugh in delight.
Classics shine, but with a flair,
Bringing chuckles everywhere we dare!

Each pin a legend, in colors bold,
Tales of laughter, proudly told.
So here's to whims, that time accounts,
With classic keepsakes, life surmounts!

www.ingramcontent.com/pod-product-compliance
Lightning Source LLC
Chambersburg PA
CBHW060135230426
43661CB00003B/431